technology of the
industrial
revolution

technology of the industrial revolution

Edited by Margaret Vallencourt

Britannica
Educational Publishing

IN ASSOCIATION WITH

ROSEN
EDUCATIONAL SERVICES

YA
609.03
TEC

First Edition

Britannica Educational Publishing
J.E. Luebering: Director, Core Reference Group
Anthony L. Green: Editor, Compton's by Britannica

Rosen Publishing
Christine Poolos: Editor
Nelson Sá: Art Director
Nicole Russo: Designer
Cindy Reiman: Photography Manager
Karen Huang: Photo Researcher

Library of Congress Cataloging-in-Publication Data

Technology of the industrial revolution / edited by Margaret Vallencourt. — First edition.
    pages cm. — (The history of technology)
  Includes bibliographical references and index.
  ISBN 978-1-68048-275-1 (library bound)
 1. Inventions—History—19th century—Juvenile literature. 2. Technology—History—19th century—Juvenile literature. 3. Technological innovations—History—19th century—Juvenile literature.
4. Industries—History—19th century—Juvenile literature. 5. Industrial revolution—Juvenile litera-ture. I. Vallencourt, Margaret, editor.
  T48.T44 2016
  609.03—dc23
                                                                                          2015018792
Manufactured in the United States of America

Photo credits: Cover, p. 3 Fazer44/Moment/Getty Images; pp. 5, 24, 30-31 © Photos.com/ Jupiterimages; pp. 6 (top), 39, 54, 63, 69 Science & Society Picture Library/Getty Images; pp. 6 (bottom), 46, 70 Library of Congress Prints and Photographs Division; p. 9 Danita Delimont/Gallo Images/Getty Images; pp. 13, 53, 60-61, 82-83 Print Collector/Hulton Archive/Getty Images; pp. 17, 40-41 © Photos.com/Thinkstock; p. 20 Private Collection/Bridgeman Images; p. 22 Courtesy of the Scottish National Portrait Gallery, Edinburgh; p. 36 British Crown copyright, Science Museum, London; pp. 48-49 De Agostini Picture Library/Getty Images; p. 56 Private Colllection/© Look and Learn/Bridgeman Images; p. 58 Encyclopaedia Britannica, Inc.; p. 67 Courtesy of CSX Transportation Inc.; pp. 74-75 FPG/Archive Photos/Getty Images; pp. 76-77 Collection de la Société Francaiçe de Photographie, Paris; p. 78 Apic/Hulton Archive/Getty Images; pp. 86-87, 95 Universal Images Group/ Getty Images; p. 91 Popperfoto/Getty Images; p. 93 Stock Montage/Archive Photos/Getty Images; p. 97 Hulton Archive/Getty Images; p. 99 Library of Congress, Washington, D.C. (digital no. 3b11564); interior pages background image BMCL/Shutterstock.com

Contents

Introduction

Technology is the process by which human beings fashion tools and machines to change, manipulate, and control their environment. In the modern world technology is all around. Automobiles, computers, nuclear power, spacecraft, and X-ray cameras are all examples of technological advances.

The Industrial Revolution began when the first factories were established in England in about 1740 to produce textiles. Within 100 years poorly made woolen goods were largely replaced by cotton goods, especially after the invention of the cotton gin by the American Eli Whitney in 1793. The steam engine, introduced in the early 18th century, became the principal power source for factories and later, with the development of the steam locomotive, for transportation. Guns with interchangeable parts replaced handcrafted weapons. Mass production of many products—compared to those produced by individual craftsmen—was made possible with the help of new machine tools.

The Industrial Revolution had a profound impact on society. For instance, the factory system changed people's way of life. It destroyed the guilds and the role of the artisan. Labor became a commodity that often exploited the men, women, and children who worked tediously in the factories.

A woman operates a cotton weaving bobbin and fly frame. During the Industrial Revolution, great advances in transportation, agriculture, and manufacturing changed society in remarkable ways.

The steam engine, which at first increased the power available beyond that of animals, soon also powered many labor-saving devices such as the sewing machine and the mechanical reaper. Initially this led to large-scale unemployment. Yet the pace of innovation and technology kept quickening.

In North America the early building of ship canals was supplanted by railroads and the erection of many bridges. Everywhere sailing ships were replaced by larger, faster, and more reliable steamships. The telegraph allowed for rapid communication. Postal services were initiated. There was growing pride in such 19th-century achievements as the Eiffel Tower in Paris, the Brooklyn Bridge in New York City, the smoking steelworks of Pittsburgh, and the transcontinental railroad.

With the invention of electric generators and motors and Thomas Edison's light bulb, electric power entered home and factory. Steel replaced iron for buildings and allowed the erection of skyscrapers. The invention of the internal-combustion engine led to the arrival of the automobile.

This in turn fostered the search for petroleum. Chemical research provided the impetus for new industries. The telephone was invented by Alexander Graham Bell in 1886. Farm machinery eased the hard life on the farm and reduced the number of people needed to feed the rest of the population.

Weapons also changed. First the rifled gun barrel was introduced, then the explosive shell that made old fortifications obsolete, and finally the machine gun. This changed large-scale warfare from individual battles to a broad front with millions of soldiers opposing each other by World War I.

Formal education in technology prospered with the establishment of engineering colleges throughout the world. By the end of the 19th century, the world had changed. In the developed nations agricultural societies had been replaced by industrial societies.

This volume examines technological developments during the era of the Industrial Revolution. This period advanced society in ways not seen until the advent of the digital revolution. A brief history of the Industrial Revolution first provides contextual background; technological achievements within individual classifications such as power, textiles, transport and communications, and other industries follow; and the volume concludes with changes to labor and the workplace that were brought about by the Industrial Revolution.

THE INDUSTRIAL REVOLUTION

Most products people in the industrialized nations use today are turned out swiftly by the process of mass production, by people (and sometimes by robots) working on assembly lines using power-driven machines. People of ancient and medieval times had no such products. They had to spend long, tedious hours of hand labor even on simple objects. The energy, or power, they employed in work came almost wholly from their own and animals' muscles. The Industrial Revolution is the name given the movement in which machines changed people's way of life as well as their methods of manufacture.

About the time of the American Revolution (1775–1783), the people of England began to use machines to make cloth and steam engines to run the machines. A little later they invented

Prior to the Industrial Revolution, every village had its tradesmen. Masons, carpenters, shopkeepers, and tailors worked independently.

locomotives. Productivity began a spectacular climb. By 1850 most Englishmen were laboring in industrial towns and Great Britain had become the workshop of the world. From Britain the Industrial Revolution spread gradually throughout Europe and to the United States.

CHANGES THAT LED TO THE REVOLUTION

The most important of the changes that brought about the Industrial Revolution were (1) the invention of machines to do the work of hand tools; (2) the use of steam, and later of other kinds of power, in place of the muscles of human beings and of animals; and (3) the adoption of the factory system.

It is almost impossible to imagine what the world would be like if the effects of the Industrial Revolution were swept away. Electric lights would go out. Automobiles and airplanes would vanish. Telephones, radios, and television would disappear. Most of the abundant stocks on the shelves of department stores would be gone. The children of the poor would have little or no schooling and would work from dawn to dark on the farm or in the home. Before machines were invented, work by children as well as by adults was needed in order to provide enough food, clothing, and shelter for all.

The Industrial Revolution came gradually. It happened in a short span of time, however, when measured against the centuries people had worked entirely by hand. Until John Kay invented the flying shuttle for looms in 1733 and James Hargreaves the spinning jenny 31 years later, the making of yarn and the weaving of cloth had been much the same for thousands of years. By 1800 a host of new and faster processes were in use in both manufacture and transportation.

This relatively sudden change in the way people live deserves to be called a revolution. It differs from a political revolution in its greater effects on the lives of people and in not coming to an end, as, for example, did the French Revolution.

Instead, the Industrial Revolution grew more powerful each year as new inventions and manufacturing processes added to the efficiency of machines and increased productivity. Indeed, since World War I the mechanization of industry increased so enormously that another revolution in production is said to have taken place.

GUILDS

In every large town in Europe during the Middle Ages, working men of each trade were members of associations called craft guilds. Guilds regulated their occupations and preserved a monopoly. In Paris, London, and other large cities there were as many as 50 or more guilds by the 14th century.

Guild rules provided that nonmembers could not practice the trade within the town. In some places a worker could become a member as soon as he showed the required degree of skill. In other places membership was difficult to obtain. It went only to sons or sons-in-law of members or could be purchased only at a high price.

The guilds required standards of quality in articles made and sold by their members, and penalties were invoked

(continued on the next page)

(continued from the previous page)

for inferior merchandise. For example, the weavers' guild required a certain number of threads to the inch in standard cloths. Hours of labor were regulated, and work at night and on holidays was prohibited. In later times the insistence on obsolete standards and processes handicapped industrial development. This led to a shifting of manufactures to villages and to new towns where guilds were not established.

Other rules provided for mutual help, including care of sick or needy members and members' widows and orphans. Once a year or more often members gathered for a feast. Since the members of a craft usually lived on the same street, the guild was also a center of social interest for its members.

EXPANDING COMMERCE AFFECTS INDUSTRY

Commerce and industry have always been closely related. Sometimes one is ahead and sometimes the other, but the one behind is always trying to catch up. Beginning about 1400, world commerce grew and changed so greatly that writers sometimes use the term *commercial revolution* to describe the economic progress of the next three and a half centuries.

Many factors helped bring about this revolution in trade. The Crusades opened up the riches of the East to Western Europe. America was discovered, and European nations began to acquire rich colonies there and elsewhere.

New trade routes were opened. The strong central governments which replaced the feudal system began to protect and help their merchants. Trading firms, such as the British East India Company, were chartered by governments. Larger ships were built, and flourishing cities grew up.

With the expansion of trade, more money was needed. Large-scale commerce could not be carried on by barter, as much of the earlier

An official of the East India Company rides in a procession.

trade had been. Gold and silver from the New World helped meet this need. Banks and credit systems developed. By the end of the 17th century Europe had a large accumulation of capital. Money had to be available before machinery and steam engines could come into wide use, for they were costly to manufacture and install.

By 1750 large quantities of goods were being exchanged among the European nations, and there was a demand for more goods than were being produced. England was the leading commercial nation, and the manufacture of cloth was its leading industry.

ORGANIZING PRODUCTION

Several systems of making goods had grown up by the time of the Industrial Revolution. In country districts families produced most of the food, clothing, and other articles they used, as they had done for centuries. In the cities merchandise was made in shops much like those of the medieval craftsmen, and manufacturing was strictly regulated by the guilds and by the government. The goods made in these shops, though of high quality, were limited and costly.

The merchants needed cheaper items, as well as larger quantities, for their growing trade. As early as the 15th century they already had begun to go outside the cities, beyond the reach of the hampering regulations, and to establish another system of producing goods.

FROM COTTAGE INDUSTRY TO FACTORY

Before the Industrial Revolution introduced the factory system, many goods were produced using a system known as cottage industry. Cloth merchants, for instance, would buy raw wool from the sheep owners, have it spun into yarn by farmers' wives, and take it to country weavers to be made into textiles. These country weavers could manufacture the cloth more cheaply than city craftsmen could because they got part of their living from their gardens or small farms.

The merchants would then collect the cloth and give it out again to finishers and dyers. Thus, they controlled cloth making from start to finish. Similar methods of organizing and controlling the process of manufacture came to prevail in other industries, such as the nail, cutlery, and leather goods.

Some writers call this the putting-out system. Others call it the domestic system because the work was done in the home (domestic comes from the Latin word for home). Another term is cottage industry, for most of the workers belonged to the class of farm laborers known as cotters and carried on the work in their cottages.

(continued on the next page)

(continued from the previous page)

The Art of Stocking-Frame-Work-Knitting.

Engrav'd for the Universal Magazine 1750 for J. Hinton at the Kings. Arms in S.ᵗ Pauls Church Yard LONDON.

In the cottage industry system, goods such as woven textiles were produced in the home.

This system of industry had several advantages over older systems. It gave the merchant a large supply of manufactured articles at a low price. It also enabled him to order the particular kinds of items that he needed for his markets. It provided employment for every member of a craft worker's family and gave jobs to skilled workers who had no capital to start businesses for themselves. A few merchants who had enough capital had gone a step further. They brought workers together under one roof and supplied them with spinning wheels and looms or with the implements of other trades. These establishments were factories, though they bear slight resemblance to the factories of today.

WHY THE REVOLUTION BEGAN IN ENGLAND

English merchants were leaders in developing a commerce which increased the demand for more goods. The expansion in trade had made it possible to accumulate capital to use in industry. A cheaper system of production had grown up which was largely free from regulation.

There also were new ideas in England that aided the movement. One of these was the growing interest in scientific investigation and invention. Another was the doctrine of laissez-faire, or letting business alone. This doctrine had been growing in favor throughout the 18th century. It was especially popular after Scottish philosopher and political economist Adam Smith argued powerfully for it in his great work *The Wealth of Nations* (1776).

For centuries the craft guilds and the government had controlled commerce and industry down to the smallest detail. Now many Englishmen had come to believe that it was better to let business be regulated by the free play of supply and demand rather than by laws. Thus, the English government for the most part kept its hands off and left business free to adopt the new inventions and the methods of production that were best suited to them.

Scottish philosopher and economist Adam Smith.

The most important of the machines that ushered in the Industrial Revolution were invented in the last third of the 18th century. Earlier in the century, however, three inventions had been made which opened the way for the later machines. One was the crude, slow-moving steam engine built by Thomas Newcomen (1705), which was used to pump water out of mines. The second was Kay's flying shuttle (1733). It enabled one person to handle a wide loom more rapidly than two persons could operate it before. The third was a frame for spinning cotton thread with rollers, first set up by Lewis Paul and John Wyatt (1741). Their invention was not commercially practical, but it was the first step toward solving the problem of machine spinning.

The Industrial Revolution eventually spread to other parts of Europe and to the United States. France and Belgium were slow to start and less invested in technology. The United States did not have enough capital to buy the machinery and put up the buildings needed. A start in manufacturing, however, was made in New England in 1790 by Samuel Slater. An employee of Arkwright's spinning mills, Slater came to the United States in 1789. He was hired by Moses Brown of Providence, R.I., to build a mill on the Pawtucket, or Seekonk, River. English laws forbade export of either the

A marked improvement on its predecessors, Thomas Newcomen's steam engine was a reliable workhorse. But it was not the model of efficiency: It worked at only 12 strokes a minute.

new machinery or plans for making it. Slater designed the machine from memory and built a mill which started operation in 1790. When the Napoleonic wars and the War of 1812 upset commerce and made English products difficult to obtain, more American investors began to build factories.

One result of the important advances made in industry from the Industrial Revolution was what is known as the Second Industrial Revolution. New scientific knowledge was applied to industry as scientists and engineers unlocked the secrets of physics and chemistry. Great new industries were founded on this scientific advance: steel, chemicals, and petroleum benefited from new understandings of chemistry; breakthroughs in the study of electricity and magnetism provided the basis for a large electrical industry. These new industries were larger and more productive than any industries existing before. Germany and the United States became the leaders, and by the end of the 19th century they were challenging Great Britain in the world market for industrial goods.

2

POWER TECHNOLOGY

O ne outstanding feature of the Industrial Revolution was the advance in power technology. At the beginning of this period, the major sources of power available to industry and any other potential consumer were animate energy and the power of wind and water, the only exception of any significance being the atmospheric steam engines that had been installed for pumping purposes, mainly in coal mines. It is to be emphasized that this use of steam power was exceptional and remained so for most industrial purposes until well into the 19th century. Steam did not simply replace other sources of power: It transformed them.

The same sort of scientific inquiry that led to the development of the steam engine was also applied to the traditional sources of inanimate energy, with the result that both waterwheels and windmills were improved in design and efficiency. Numerous engineers contributed to the refinement of waterwheel construction, and by the middle of the 19th century new designs made possible increases in the speed of revolution of the waterwheel and thus prepared the way for the emergence of the water turbine, which is still an extremely efficient device for converting energy.

WINDMILLS

Meanwhile, British windmill construction was improved considerably by the refinements of sails and by the self-correcting device of the fantail, which kept the sails pointed into the wind. Spring sails replaced the traditional canvas rig of the windmill with the equivalent of a modern venetian blind, the shutters of which could be opened or closed, to let the wind pass through or to provide a surface upon which its pressure could be exerted. Sail design was further improved with the "patent" sail in 1807. In mills equipped with these sails, the shutters were controlled on all the sails simultaneously by a lever inside the mill connected by rod linkages through the windshaft with the bar operating the movement of the shutters on each sweep. The control could be made more fully automatic by hanging weights on the lever in the mill to determine the maximum wind pressure beyond which the shutters would open and spill the wind. Conversely, counter-weights could be attached to keep the shutters in the open position. With these and other modifications, British windmills adapted to the increasing demands on power technology. But the use of wind power declined sharply in the 19th century with the spread of steam and the increasing scale of power utilization. Windmills that had satisfactorily provided power for small-scale industrial processes were unable to compete with the production of large-scale steam-powered mills.

STEAM ENGINES

Although the qualification regarding older sources of power is important, steam became the characteristic and ubiquitous power source of the British Industrial Revolution. Little development took place in the Newcomen atmospheric engine until James Watt patented a separate condenser in 1769, but from that point onward the steam engine underwent almost continuous improvements for more than a century. Watt's separate condenser was the outcome of his work on a model of a Newcomen engine that was being used in a University of Glasgow laboratory. Watt's inspiration was to separate the two actions of heating the cylinder with hot steam and cooling it to condense the steam for every stroke of the engine. By keeping the cylinder permanently hot and the condenser permanently cold, a great economy on energy used could be effected. This brilliantly simple idea could not be immediately incorporated in a full-scale engine because the engineering of such machines had hitherto been crude and defective. The backing of a Birmingham industrialist, Matthew Boulton, with his resources of capital and technical competence, was needed to convert the idea into a commercial success. Between 1775 and 1800, the period over which Watt's patents were extended, the Boulton and Watt partnership produced some 500 engines, which despite their high cost in relation to a Newcomen engine were eagerly acquired by the tin-mining industrialists of Cornwall and other power users who badly needed a more economic and reliable source of energy.

During the quarter of a century in which Boulton and Watt exercised their virtual monopoly over the manufacture of improved steam engines, they introduced many important refinements. Basically they converted the engine from a single-acting (i.e., applying power only on the downward stroke of the piston) atmospheric pumping machine into a versatile prime mover that was double-acting

James Watt invented the separate condenser for the steam engine around 1765. He patented the condenser in 1768.

and could be applied to rotary motion, thus driving the wheels of industry. The rotary action engine was quickly adopted by British textile manufacturer Sir Richard Arkwright for use in a cotton mill. Many other industries followed in exploring the possibilities of steam power, and it soon became widely used.

Watt's patents had the temporary effect of restricting the development of high-pressure steam, necessary in such major power applications as the locomotive. This development came quickly once these patents lapsed in 1800. The Cornish engineer Richard Trevithick introduced higher steam pressures, achieving an unprecedented pressure of 145 pounds per square inch (10 kilograms per square centimeter) in 1802 with an experimental engine at Coalbrookdale, which worked safely and efficiently. Almost simultaneously, the versatile American engineer Oliver Evans built the first high-pressure steam engine in the United States, using, like Trevithick, a cylindrical boiler with an internal fire plate and flue. High-pressure steam engines rapidly became popular in America, partly as a result of Evans' initiative and partly because very few Watt-type low-pressure engines crossed the Atlantic. Trevithick quickly applied his engine to a vehicle, making the first successful steam locomotive for the Penydarren tramroad in South Wales in 1804. The success, however, was technological rather than commercial because the locomotive fractured the cast iron track of the tramway: the age of the railroad had to await further development both of the permanent way and of the locomotive.

STEAM ENGINE OPERATION

In a typical steam engine, steam flows in a double-acting cylinder. The flow can be controlled by a single-sliding D valve. When the piston is in the left side of the cylinder, high-pressure steam is admitted from the steam chest. At the same time, the expanded steam from the right side of the cylinder escapes through the exhaust port. As the piston moves to the right, the valve slides over both the exhaust ports and ports connecting the steam chest and the cylinder, preventing more steam from entering the cylinder. The high-pressure steam within the cylinder then expands. The steam expansion pushes the piston rod, which is usually connected to a crank in order to produce rotary motion. When the valve is all the way to the left, steam in the left-hand portion of the cylinder escapes as exhaust. At the same time, the right-hand portion of the cylinder is filled with fresh high-pressure steam from the steam chest. This steam drives the piston to the left. The position of the sliding D valve can be varied, depending on the position of an eccentric crank on the flywheel.

Valve gearing plays a major role in a steam locomotive because a wide range of effort is required of the engine. If the load on the engine is increased, the engine would tend to slow down. The engine governor moves the location of the eccentric in order to increase the length of time during which steam is admitted to the cylinder. As more steam is admitted, the engine output increases. The efficiency of the engine decreases, however, because the steam can no longer expand fully.

Although the D-slide valve is a simple mechanism, the pressure exerted by the high-pressure steam on the back of the sliding valve causes significant friction losses and wear. This can be avoided by using separate cylindrical spring-loaded spool valves enclosed in their own chamber, as first proposed by George Corliss in 1849.

Arrangements more complicated than a simple eccentric are needed if a steam engine has to run at different speeds and loads as well as forward and backward, as does a steam locomotive. This leads to a complex arrangement of sliding valve levers, known as the valve gear.

Meanwhile, the stationary steam engine advanced steadily to meet an ever-widening market of industrial requirements. High-pressure steam led to the development of the large beam pumping engines with a complex sequence of valve actions, which became universally known as Cornish engines; their distinctive characteristic was the cutoff of steam injection before the stroke was complete in order to allow the steam to do work by expanding. These engines were used all over the world for heavy pumping duties, often being shipped out and installed by Cornish engineers. Trevithick himself spent many years improving pumping engines in Latin America. Cornish engines, however, were probably most common in Cornwall itself, where they were used in large numbers in the tin and copper mining industries.

Another consequence of high-pressure steam was the practice of compounding, of using the steam twice or more at descending pressures before it was finally condensed or exhausted. The technique was first applied by Arthur Woolf, a Cornish mining engineer, who by 1811 had produced a very satisfactory and efficient compound beam engine with a high-pressure cylinder placed alongside the low-pressure cylinder, with both piston rods attached to the same pin of the parallel motion, which was a parallelogram of rods connecting the piston to the beam, patented by Watt in 1784. In 1845 John McNaught introduced an alternative form of compound beam engine, with the high-pressure cylinder on the opposite end of the beam from the low-pressure cylinder and working with a shorter stroke. This became a very popular design.

Various other methods of compounding steam engines were adopted, and the practice became increasingly widespread; in the second half of the 19th century triple- or quadruple-expansion engines were being used in industry and marine propulsion. By this time also the conventional beam-type vertical engine adopted by Newcomen and retained by Watt began to be replaced by horizontal-cylinder designs. Beam engines remained in use for some purposes until the eclipse of the reciprocating steam engine in the 20th century, and other types of vertical engines remained popular, but for both large and small duties the engine designs with horizontal cylinders became by far the most common.

A demand for power to generate electricity stimulated new thinking about the steam engine in the 1880s. The problem was that of achieving a sufficiently high rotational speed to make the dynamos function efficiently. Such speeds were beyond the range of the normal

James Watt's steam engine displaced Thomas Newcomen's slow, clumsy steam pumping engine. Watt's engine featured a flywheel, a crank, and a steam governor.

reciprocating engine (i.e., with a piston moving backward and forward in a cylinder). Designers began to investigate the possibilities of radical modifications to the reciprocating engine to achieve the speeds desired or of devising a steam engine working on a completely different principle.

In the first category, one solution was to enclose the working parts of the engine and force a lubricant around them under pressure. The Willans engine design, for instance, was of this type and was widely adopted in early British power stations. Another important modification in the reciprocating design was the uniflow engine, which increased efficiency by exhausting steam from ports in the center of the cylinder instead of requiring it to change its direction of flow in the cylinder with every movement of the piston. Full success in achieving a high-speed steam engine, however, depended on the steam turbine, a design of such novelty that it constituted a major technological innovation. This was invented by Sir Charles Parsons in 1884. By passing steam through the blades of a series of rotors of gradually increasing size (to allow for the expansion of the steam) the energy of the steam was converted to very rapid circular motion, which was ideal for generating electricity.

Many refinements have since been made in turbine construction and the size of turbines has been vastly increased, but the basic principles remain the same, and this method still provides the main source of electric power except in those areas in which the mountainous terrain permits the economic generation of hydroelectric power by water turbines. Even the most modern nuclear power plants use steam turbines because technology has not yet solved the problem of transforming nuclear energy directly into electricity. In marine propulsion, too, the steam turbine remains an important source of power despite competition from the internal-combustion engine.

ELECTRICITY

The development of electricity as a source of power preceded this conjunction with steam power late in the 19th century. The pioneering work had been done by an international collection of scientists including Benjamin Franklin of Pennsylvania, Alessandro Volta of the University of Pavia, Italy, and Michael Faraday of Britain. It was the latter who had demonstrated the nature of the elusive relationship between electricity and magnetism in 1831, and his experiments provided the point of departure for both the mechanical generation of electric current, previously available only from chemical reactions within voltaic piles or batteries, and the utilization of such current in electric motors. Both the mechanical generator and the motor depend on the rotation of a continuous coil of conducting wire between the poles of a strong magnet: turning the

The axial flow turbine used high-pressure steam to turn fast enough to produce electricity on a large scale.

coil produces a current in it, while passing a current through the coil causes it to turn. Both generators and motors underwent substantial development in the middle decades of the 19th century. In particular, French, German, Belgian, and Swiss engineers evolved the most satisfactory forms of armature (the coil of wire) and produced the dynamo, which made the large-scale generation of electricity commercially feasible.

The next problem was that of finding a market. In Britain, with its now well-established tradition of steam power, coal, and coal gas, such a market was not immediately obvious. But in continental Europe and North America there was more scope for experiment. In the United States Thomas Edison applied his inventive genius to finding fresh uses for electricity, and his development of the carbon-filament lamp showed how this form of energy could rival gas as a domestic illuminant. The problem had been that electricity had been used successfully for large installations such as lighthouses in

Michael Faraday demonstrated the connection between electricity and magnetism at a lecture at the Royal Institution on January 23, 1846. Faraday's research established the field theory of electromagnetism.

which arc lamps had been powered by generators on the premises, but no way of subdividing the electric light into many small units had been devised. The principle of the filament lamp was that a thin conductor could be made incandescent by an electric current, provided that it was sealed in a vacuum to keep it from burning out. Edison and the English chemist Sir Joseph Swan experimented with various materials for the filament and both chose carbon. The result was a highly successful small lamp, which could be varied in size for any sort of requirement.

It is relevant that the success of the carbon-filament lamp did not immediately mean the supersession of gas lighting. Coal gas had first been used for lighting by William Murdock at his home in Redruth, Cornwall, where he was the agent for the Boulton and Watt company, in 1792. When he moved to the headquarters of the firm at Soho in Birmingham in 1798, Matthew Boulton authorized him to experiment in lighting the buildings there by gas, and gas lighting was subsequently adopted by firms and towns all over Britain in the first half of the 19th century. Lighting was normally provided by a fishtail jet of burning gas, but under the stimulus of competition from electric lighting the quality of gas lighting was greatly enhanced by the invention of the gas mantle.

Thus improved, gas lighting remained popular for some forms of street lighting until the middle of the 20th century.

Lighting alone could not provide an economical market for electricity because its use was confined to the hours of darkness. Successful commercial generation depended upon the development of other uses for electricity and particularly on electric traction. The popularity of urban electric tramways and the adoption of electric traction on subway systems such as the London Underground thus coincided with the widespread construction of generating equipment in the late 1880s and 1890s. The subsequent spread of this form of energy is one of the most remarkable technological success stories of the 20th century, but most of the basic techniques of generation, distribution, and utilization had been mastered by the end of the 19th century.

INTERNAL-COMBUSTION ENGINE

The internal-combustion engine emerged in the 19th century as a result both of greater scientific understanding of the principles of thermodynamics and of a search by engineers for a substitute for steam power in certain circumstances.

In an internal-combustion engine the fuel is burned in the engine: the cannon provided an early model of a single-stroke engine, and several persons had experimented with gunpowder as a means of driving a piston in a cylinder. The major problem was that of finding a suitable fuel, and the secondary problem was that of igniting the fuel in an enclosed space to produce an action that could be easily and quickly repeated. The first problem was solved in the mid-19th century by the introduction of town gas supplies, but the second problem proved more intractable as it was difficult to maintain ignition evenly.

The first successful gas engine was made by Étienne Lenoir in Paris in 1859. It was modeled closely on a horizontal steam engine, with an explosive mixture of gas and air ignited by an electric spark on alternate sides of the piston when it was in midstroke position. Although technically satisfactory, the engine was expensive to operate, and it was not until the refinement introduced by the German inventor Nikolaus Otto in 1878 that the gas engine became a commercial success. Otto adopted the four-stroke cycle of induction-compression-firing-exhaust that has been known by his name ever since. Gas engines became extensively used for small industrial establishments, which could thus dispense with the upkeep of a boiler necessary in any steam plant, however small.

PETROLEUM

The economic potential for the internal-combustion engine lay in the need for a light locomotive engine. This could not be provided by the gas engine, depending on a piped supply of town gas, any more than by the steam engine, with its need for a cumbersome boiler. By using alternative fuels derived from oil, the internal-combustion engine took to wheels, with momentous consequences.

In 1859 the oil industry took on new significance when Edwin L. Drake bored successfully through 69 feet (21 meters) of rock to strike oil in Pennsylvania, thus inaugurating the search for and exploitation of the deep oil resources of the world. While world supplies of oil expanded dramatically, the main demand was at first for the kerosene, the middle fraction distilled from the raw material, which was used as the fuel in oil lamps. The most volatile fraction of the oil, gasoline, remained an embarrassing waste product until it was discovered that this could be burned in a light internal-combustion engine; the result was an ideal prime mover for vehicles.

The way was prepared for this development by the success of oil engines burning cruder

The oil boom in the United States commenced with Edwin Drake's drilling through Pennsylvania rock to strike oil in 1859. This achievement sparked business in the drilling, refining, and selling of oil.

fractions of oil. Kerosene-burning oil engines, modeled closely on existing gas engines, had emerged in the 1870s, and by the late 1880s engines using the vapor of heavy oil in a jet of compressed air and working on the Otto cycle had become an attractive proposition for light duties in places too isolated to use town gas.

The greatest refinements in the heavy-oil engine are associated with the work of Rudolf Diesel of Germany, who took out his first patents in 1892. Working from thermodynamic principles of minimizing heat losses, Diesel devised an engine in which the very high compression of the air in the cylinder secured the spontaneous ignition of the oil when it was injected in a carefully determined quantity. This ensured high thermal efficiency, but it also made necessary a heavy structure because of the high compression maintained, and also a rather rough performance at low speeds compared with other oil engines. It was therefore not immediately suitable for locomotive purposes, but Diesel went on improving his engine and in the 20th century it became an important form of vehicular propulsion.

Meantime the light high-speed gasoline (petrol) engine predominated. The first applications of the new engine to locomotion were made in Germany, where Gottlieb Daimler and Karl Benz equipped the first motorcycle and the first motorcar respectively with engines of their own design in 1885. Benz's "horseless carriage" became the prototype of the modern automobile, the development and consequences of which can be more conveniently considered in relation to the revolution in transport.

By the end of the 19th century, the internal-combustion engine was challenging the steam engine in many industrial and transport applications. It is notable that, whereas the pioneers of the steam engine had been almost all Britons, most of the innovators in internal combustion were continental Europeans and Americans. The transition, indeed, reflects the general change in international leadership in the Industrial Revolution, with Britain being gradually displaced from its position of unchallenged superiority in industrialization and technological innovation. A similar transition occurred in the

Karl Benz built the first horseless carriage, powered by an internal-combustion engine, in 1885.

theoretical understanding of heat engines: It was the work of the Frenchman Sadi Carnot and other scientific investigators that led to the new science of thermodynamics, rather than that of the British engineers who had most practical experience of the engines on which the science was based.

The success of these machines stimulated speculation about alternative sources of power, including the hot-air engine, for which a Scotsman, Robert Stirling, took out a patent in 1816. The hot-air engine depends for its power on the expansion and displacement of air inside a cylinder, heated by the external and continuous combustion of the fuel. Even before the exposition of the laws of thermodynamics, Stirling had devised a cycle of heat transfer that was ingenious and economical. Various constructional problems limited the size of hot-air engines to very small units, so that although they were widely used for driving fans and similar light duties before the availability of the electric motor, they did not assume great technological significance. But the economy and comparative cleanness of the hot-air engine were making it once more the subject of intensive research in the early 1970s.

The transformation of power technology in the Industrial Revolution had repercussions throughout industry and society. In the first place, the demand for fuel stimulated the coal industry, which had already grown rapidly by the beginning of the 18th century, into continuing expansion and innovation. The steam engine, which enormously increased the need for coal, contributed significantly toward obtaining it by providing more efficient mine pumps and, eventually, improved ventilating equipment.

INVENTIONS IN THE TEXTILE INDUSTRY

Textile manufacturing is one of the largest industries in the world today. Whether done in the home as a cottage industry or in large factories, most countries produce fibers and textiles for both domestic consumption and for export. Even in countries that are considered underdeveloped, the introduction of modern technology has enabled the work force to mass-produce textiles for the world market and the country to compete successfully with the more industrialized societies. The textile industry we know today is in large part a result of technological advances made during the Industrial Revolution.

SPINNING AND WEAVING MACHINERY

As John Kay's flying shuttle sped up weaving, the demand for cotton yarn increased. Many inventors set to work to improve the spinning wheel. James Hargreaves, a weaver who was also a carpenter, patented his spinning jenny in 1770. It enabled one worker to run eight spindles instead of one.

About the same time Richard Arkwright developed his water frame, a machine for spinning with rollers operated by water power. In 1779 Samuel Crompton, a spinner, combined

Cotton manufacturers could produce better yarn more quickly with the use of a spinning mule.

Hargreaves's jenny and Arkwright's roller frame into a spinning machine, called a mule. It produced thread of greater fineness and strength than the jenny or the roller frame. Since the roller frame and the mule were large and heavy,

SAMUEL CROMPTON'S SPINNING MULE

As a youth in England, Samuel Crompton (1753–1827) spun cotton on a spinning jenny for his family; its defects inspired him to try to invent a better device. In 1779, after devoting

Samuel Crompton combined elements of Thomas Kay's flying shuttle and James Hargreaves's spinning jenny to create the spinning mule.

all his spare time and money to the effort, he produced a machine that simultaneously drew out and gave the final twisting to the cotton fibers fed into it, reproducing mechanically the actions of hand spinning. Probably the machine was called a mule because it was a cross between the machines invented by Sir Richard Arkwright and James Hargreaves.

Demand for Crompton's yarn was heavy, but he could not afford a patent. He therefore revealed the machine's secret to a number of manufacturers on the promise that they would pay him. All he received was £60. Years later (in 1812), when there were at least 360 mills using 4,600,000 mule spindles, Parliament granted him £5,000. He used it to enter business, unsuccessfully, first as a bleacher and then as a cotton merchant and spinner.

it became the practice to install them in mills, where they could be run by water power. They were tended by women and children.

These improvements in spinning machinery called for further improvements in weaving. In 1785 Edmund Cartwright patented a power loom. In spite of the need for it, weaving machinery came into use very slowly. First, many improvements had to be made before the loom was satisfactory. Second, the hand weavers violently opposed its adoption because it threw many of them out of work. Those who got jobs in the factories were obliged to take the same pay as unskilled workers. Thus, some people rioted, smashed the machines, and tried to prevent their use. The power loom was

Not everyone appreciated the direction technology was taking. In 1768 a group of threatened spinners broke into James Hargreaves's home and destroyed his spinning jennys.

only coming into wide operation in the cotton industry by 1813. It did not completely replace the hand loom in weaving cotton until 1850. It was not well adapted to the making of some woolens. As late as 1880 many hand looms were still in use for weaving woolen cloth.

Many other machines contributed to the progress of the textile industry. In 1785 Thomas Bell of Glasgow, Scot., invented cylinder printing of cotton goods. This was a great improvement on block printing. It made successive impressions of a design "join up" and did the work more rapidly and more cheaply. In 1793 the available supply of cotton was increased by American Eli Whitney's invention of the cotton gin. In 1804 J.M. Jacquard, a Frenchman, perfected a loom on which patterns might be woven in fabrics by mechanical

THE COTTON GIN

The cotton gin, a machine that cleaned cotton of its seeds, was invented in the United States by Eli Whitney in 1793. The cotton gin is an example of an invention directly called forth by an immediate demand; the mechanization of spinning in England had created a greatly expanded market for American cotton, whose production was inhibited by the slowness of

(continued on the next page)

(continued from the previous page)

Plantation slaves use a cotton gin to remove seeds from cotton. The invention may have prolonged the institution of slavery.

manual removal of the seeds from the raw fiber. Whitney, a Massachusetts Yankee visiting a friend in the South, learned of the problem and quickly solved it with a device that pulled the cotton through a set of wire teeth mounted on a revolving cylinder, the fiber passing through narrow slots in an iron breastwork too small to permit passage of the seed. The simplicity of the invention—which could be powered by man, animal, or water—caused it to be widely copied despite Whitney's patent; it is credited with fixing cotton cultivation, virtually to the exclusion of other crops, in the U.S. South and so institutionalizing slavery.

means. This loom was later adapted to the making of lace, which became available to everyone.

RAPID RISE OF THE COTTON INDUSTRY

The cotton-textile industry was the industry that, probably more than any other, gave its character to the British Industrial Revolution. The traditional dates of the Industrial Revolution bracket the period in which the processes of cotton manufacture in Britain were transformed from those of a small-scale domestic industry scattered over the towns and villages of the South Pennines into those of a large-scale, concentrated, power-driven, mechanized, factory-organized, urban industry.

The transformation was undoubtedly dramatic both to contemporaries and to posterity, and there is no doubting its immense significance in the overall pattern of British industrialization. But its importance in the history of technology should not be exaggerated. Certainly there were many interesting mechanical improvements, at least at the beginning of the transformation. The development of the spinning wheel into the spinning jenny, and the use of rollers and moving trolleys to mechanize

Innovations in cotton manufacture encouraged advances in other industries, as well. Soon, entire communities sprang up around mills.

spinning in the shape of the frame and the mule, respectively, initiated a drastic rise in the productivity of the industry. But these were secondary innovations in the sense that there were precedents for them in the experiments of the previous generation; that in any case the first British textile factory was the Derby silk mill built in 1719; and that the most far-reaching innovation in cotton manufacture was the introduction of steam power to drive carding machines, spinning machines, power looms, and printing machines.

This, however, is probably to overstate the case, and the cotton innovators should not be deprived of credit for their enterprise and ingenuity in transforming the British cotton industry and making it the model for subsequent exercises in industrialization. Not only was it copied, belatedly and slowly, by the woolen-cloth industry in Britain, but wherever other nations sought to industrialize they tried to acquire British cotton machinery and the expertise of British cotton industrialists and artisans.

One of the important consequences of the rapid rise of the British cotton industry was the dynamic stimulus it gave to other processes and industries. The rising demand for raw cotton, for example, encouraged the plantation economy of the southern United States and the introduction of Whitney's cotton gin.

ADVANCES IN FABRICATION

All operations in the fabrication of clothing were performed by hand until factory production of cloth was made possible. This development in turn stimulated the invention of the sewing machine. After several attempts, a practical machine was patented in 1830 by Barthélemy Thimonnier of Paris, who produced 80 machines to manufacture army uniforms. Thimonnier's machines, however, were destroyed by a mob of tailors who feared unemployment. Thimonnier's design used one thread; an American, Elias Howe, improved on it significantly with a lock-stitch machine that used two threads, a needle, and a shuttle. Though patented there, it was not accepted in the United States; Howe took it to England, where he sold part of his patent rights. The objections of the American tailors and seamstresses were overcome by a machine designed

Thimonnier's chain-stitch sewing machine worked by drawing thread by a barbed needle from a reel beneath the table. The thread is pulled through cloth to form a chain stitch.

in 1851 by Isaac M. Singer of Pittstown, N.Y. When the sewing machine was first introduced, it was used only for simple seams; the more complex sewing operations were still done with a hand needle. The machines before Singer's were hand-powered, but Singer quickly popularized foot-powered machines.

For many years the sewing machine was the only machine used by the clothing industry. The next major development was not until 1860, when the band-knife machine was introduced. This machine cut several thicknesses of cloth at one time. The resulting increased cutting productivity motivated the development of spreading machines to spread fabric from long bolts in lays composed of hundreds of plies of fabrics.

ADVANCES IN TRANSPORT AND COMMUNICATIONS

Transport and communications provide an example of a revolution within the Industrial Revolution, so completely were the modes transformed in the period 1750–1900. By the beginning of the 19th century, British engineers were beginning to innovate in both road- and canal-building techniques, with J.L. McAdam's inexpensive and long-wearing road surface of compacted stones and Thomas Telford's well-engineered canals. The outstanding innovation in transport, however, was the application of steam power, which occurred in three forms.

STEAM LOCOMOTIVE

First was the evolution of the railroad: the combination of the steam locomotive and a permanent travel way of metal rails. Experiments in this conjunction in the first quarter of the 19th century culminated in the Stockton & Darlington Railway, opened in 1825, and a further five years of experience with steam locomotives led to the Liverpool and Manchester Railway, which, when it opened in 1830, constituted the first fully time-tabled railway service with scheduled freight and passenger traffic relying entirely on the steam locomotive for traction. This railway was designed by George Stephenson, and the locomotives were the work of Stephenson and his son Robert, the first locomotive being the famous *Rocket*, which won a competition held by the proprietors of the railway at Rainhill, outside Liverpool, in 1829.

The opening of the Liverpool and Manchester line may fairly be regarded as the inauguration of the railway era, which continued until World War I. During this time railways were built across all the countries and continents of the world, opening up vast areas to the markets of industrial society. Locomotives increased rapidly in size and power, but the essential principles remained the same as those established by the Stephensons in the early 1830s: horizontal cylinders mounted beneath a multitubular boiler with a firebox at the rear and a tender carrying supplies of water

George Stephenson's *Rocket* improved upon existing locomotive designs. *Rocket* was originally built to win a speed trial and was quickly modified to run on the Liverpool and Manchester line.

and fuel. This was the form developed from the *Rocket*, which had diagonal cylinders, being itself a stage in the transition from the vertical cylinders, often encased by the boiler, which had been typical of the earliest locomotives (except Trevithick's Penydarren engine, which had a horizontal cylinder).

Meanwhile, the construction of the permanent way underwent a corresponding improvement on that which had been common on the preceding tramroads: Wrought-iron, and eventually steel, rails replaced the cast-iron rails, which cracked easily under a steam locomotive, and well-aligned track with easy gradients and substantial supporting civil-engineering works became a commonplace of the railroads of the world.

ROAD LOCOMOTIVE

The second form in which steam power was applied to transport was that of the road locomotive. There is no technical reason why this should not have enjoyed a success equal to that of the railway engine, but its development was so constricted by the unsuitability of most roads and by the jealousy of other road users that it achieved general utility only for heavy traction work and such duties as road rolling. The steam traction engine, which

The steam-powered road locomotive did not enjoy success as it was originally intended. However, the machine was used widely for farming.

could be readily adapted from road haulage to power farm machines, was nevertheless a distinguished product of 19th-century steam technology.

STEAMBOATS AND SHIPS

The third application was considerably more important, because it transformed marine transport. The initial attempts to use a steam engine to power a boat were made on the Seine River in France in 1775, and several experimental steamships were built by William Symington in Britain at the turn of the 19th century. The first commercial success in steam propulsion

Robert Fulton's North River Steamboat, also known as the *Clermont*, was the first commercially succesful ship to be powered by steam engine.

for a ship, however, was that of the American Robert Fulton, whose paddle steamer the North River Steamboat, commonly known as the *Clermont* after its first overnight port, plied between New York and Albany in 1807, equipped with a Boulton and Watt engine of the modified beam or side-lever type, with two beams placed alongside the base of the engine in order to lower the center of gravity. A similar engine was installed in the Glasgow-built *Comet*, which was put in service on the Clyde in 1812 and was the first successful steamship in Europe.

All the early steamships were paddle-driven, and all were small vessels suitable only for ferry and packet duties because it was long thought

ROBERT FULTON

Robert Fulton was born on Nov. 14, 1765, on a Pennsylvania farm in what is now Fulton Township. At 21 he went to London to study art. He made friends in the scientific and engineering fields and became caught up in a series of inventions, including dredging machines, flax-spinning and rope-making devices, and a substitute for canal locks.

In 1797 he proposed the building of a submarine to the French government. It rejected his idea, but Fulton eventually

(continued on the next page)

(continued from the previous page)

built and launched *Nautilus* on his own in 1800. In Paris in 1801 he met the American minister Robert R. Livingston, who had obtained a 20-year monopoly on steamboat navigation in the state of New York. He returned to the United States as Livingston's partner to work out a practical steamboat, using an engine and boiler purchased in England from Boulton and Watt. On Aug. 17, 1807, Fulton's first steamboat, the *Clermont*, made a trial voyage—from New York Harbor, up the Hudson River, to Albany and back. The experiment was a triumph, discrediting skeptics who had called it "Fulton's folly." During the next eight years Fulton established and managed steamboat lines, and in 1814 he was commissioned by the federal government to build its first steam warship. He died in New York City on Feb. 24, 1815.

Fulton did the most to make steamboats a commercial success. Other inventors pioneered in steam navigation before him, but it was Fulton who proved that their vision and designs were practical.

that the fuel requirements of a steamship would be so large as to preclude long-distance cargo carrying. The further development of the steamship was thus delayed until the 1830s, when I.K. Brunel began to apply his ingenious and innovating mind to the problems of steamship construction. His three great steamships each marked a leap forward in technique. *The Great Western* (launched 1837), the first built specifically for oceanic service in the North Atlantic, demonstrated that the proportion of space required for fuel decreased as the total volume of the ship increased. *The Great Britain* (launched 1843) was the first large iron ship in the world and the first to be screw-propelled; its return to the port of Bristol in 1970, after a long working life and abandonment to the elements, is a remarkable testimony to the strength of its construction. *The Great Eastern* (launched 1858), with its total displacement of 18,918 tons, was by far the largest ship built in the 19th century. With a double iron hull and two sets of engines driving both a screw and paddles, this leviathan was never an economic success, but it admirably demonstrated the technical possibilities of the large iron steam-ship. By the end of the century, steamships were well on the way to displacing the sailing ship on all the main trade routes of the world.

PRINTING AND PHOTOGRAPHY

Communications were equally transformed in the 19th century. The steam engine helped to mechanize and thus to speed up the processes of papermaking and printing. In the latter case the acceleration was achieved by the introduction of the high-speed rotary press and the Linotype machine for casting type and setting it in justified lines (i.e., with

Invented by Ottmar Morgenthaler, the Linotype machine revolutionized publishing. These machines canceled the need for compositors to work letter by letter, increasing the speed and efficiency of printing.

even right-hand margins). Printing, indeed, had to undergo a technological revolution comparable to the 15th-century invention of movable type to be able to supply the greatly increasing market for the printed word.

Another important process that was to make a vital contribution to modern printing was discovered and developed in the 19th century: photography. The first photograph was taken in 1826 or 1827 by the French physicist J.N. Niepce, using a pewter plate coated with a form of bitumen that hardened on exposure. His partner L.-J.-M. Daguerre and the Englishman W.H. Fox Talbot adopted silver compounds to give light sensitivity, and the technique developed rapidly in the middle decades of

Photography advanced with the invention of the daguerreotype, as seen in this 1837 example by Daguerre, *Still Life*.

the century. By the 1890s George Eastman in the United States was manufacturing cameras and celluloid photographic film for a popular market, and the first experiments with the cinema were beginning to attract attention.

TELEGRAPHS AND TELEPHONES

The great innovations in communications technology, however, derived from electricity. The first was the electric telegraph, invented or at least made into a practical proposition for use on the developing British railway system by two British inventors, Sir William Cooke and Sir Charles Wheatstone, who collaborated on the work and took out a joint patent in 1837. Almost simultaneously, the American inventor Samuel F.B. Morse devised the signaling code that was subsequently adopted all over the world. In the next quarter of a century the continents of the world were linked telegraphically by transoceanic cables, and the

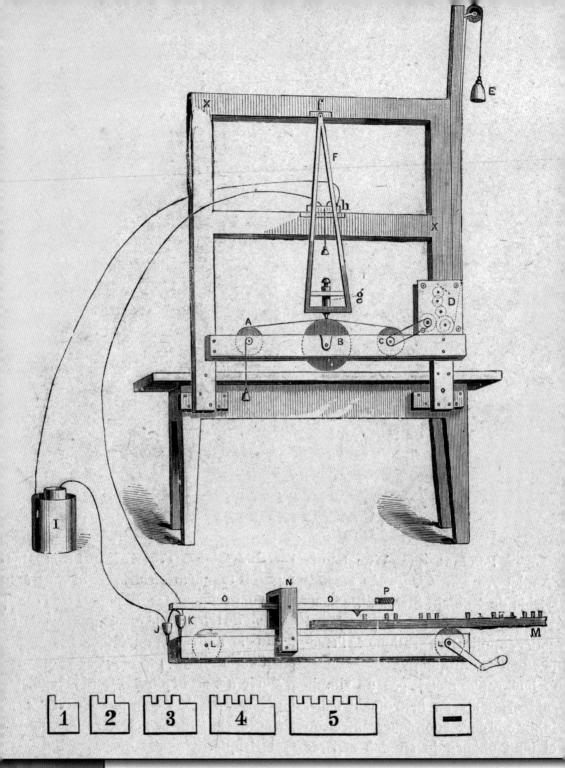

Long before the Internet, and even before the telephone, Samuel Morse connected the world with the first electric telegraph. This invention increased the speed of long-distance communication.

main political and commercial centers were brought into instantaneous communication. The telegraph system also played an important part in the opening up of the American West by providing rapid aid in the maintenance of law and order.

The electric telegraph was followed by the telephone, invented by Alexander Graham Bell in 1876 and adopted quickly for short-range oral communication in the cities of America and at a somewhat more leisurely pace in those of Europe. About the same time, theoretical work on the electromagnetic properties of light and other radiation was beginning to produce astonishing experimental results, and the possibilities of wireless telegraphy began to be explored. By the end of the century, Guglielmo Marconi had transmitted messages over many miles in Britain and was preparing the apparatus with which he made the first transatlantic radio communication on Dec. 12, 1901. The world was thus being drawn inexorably into a closer community by the spread of instantaneous communication.

5

THE DEVELOPMENT OF INDUSTRY

The Industrial Revolution was responsible for the development or advancement of several other industries, as well. These industries include metallurgy and metal trades, mechanical engineering, chemicals, agriculture, and civil engineering.

METALLURGY

Interacting closely with the power revolution was industry concerned with metallurgy and the metal trades. The development of techniques for working with iron and steel was one of the outstanding British achievements of the Industrial Revolution. The essential characteristic of this achievement was that changing the fuel of the iron and steel industry from charcoal to coal enormously increased the production of these metals. It also provided another incentive to coal production and made available the materials that were indispensable for the construction of steam engines and every other sophisticated form of machine.

IRON AND STEEL

The British iron and steel industry was freed from its reliance upon the forests as a source of charcoal and was encouraged to move toward the major coalfields. Abundant cheap iron thus became an outstanding feature of the early stages of the Industrial Revolution in Britain. Cast iron was available for bridge construction, for the framework of fireproof factories, and for other civil-engineering purposes such as Thomas Telford's novel cast-iron aqueducts. Wrought iron was available for all manner of mechanical devices requiring strength and precision.

Steel remained a comparatively rare metal until the second half of the 19th century, when the situation was transformed by the Bessemer and Siemens processes for manufacturing steel in bulk. Henry Bessemer took out the patent for his converter in 1856. It consisted of a large vessel charged with molten iron, through which cold air was blown. There was a spectacular reaction resulting from the combination

The Bessemer process, which relied on a Bessemer converter, was the first method discovered for the mass production of steel.

of impurities in the iron with oxygen in the air, and when this subsided it left mild steel in the converter.

Meanwhile, the Siemens-Martin open-hearth process was introduced in 1864, utilizing the hot waste gases of cheap fuel to heat a regenerative furnace, with the initial heat transferred to the gases circulating round the large hearth in which the reactions within the molten metal could be carefully controlled to produce steel of the quality required. The open-hearth process was gradually refined and by the end of the 19th century had overtaken the Bessemer process in the amount of steel produced. The effect of these two processes was to make steel available in bulk instead of small-scale ingots of cast crucible steel, and thenceforward steel steadily replaced wrought iron as the major commodity of the iron and steel industry.

THE OPEN-HEARTH PROCESS

The open-hearth process, also called Siemens-Martin Process, was a steelmaking technique that accounted for the major part of all steel made in the world for most of the 20th century. Seeking a means of increasing the temperature in a metallurgical furnace, William Siemens resurrected an old proposal for using the waste heat given off by the furnace. Directing the fumes from the furnace through a brick checkerwork, he heated the brick to a high temperature, then used the same pathway for the introduction of air into the furnace. The preheated air materially increased the flame temperature.

Natural gas or atomized heavy oils are used as fuel; both air and fuel are heated before combustion. The furnace is charged with liquid blast-furnace iron and steel scrap together with iron ore, limestone, dolomite, and fluxes. The furnace itself is made of highly refractory materials such as magnesite bricks for the hearths and roofs. Capacities of open-hearth furnaces are as high as 600 tons, and they are usually installed in groups, so that the massive auxiliary equipment needed to charge the furnaces and handle the liquid steel can be efficiently employed.

The ores most readily available in both Great Britain and the United States were especially well suited to the open-hearth process, the product of which proved superior to that from the Bessemer converter. Though the open-hearth process has been almost completely replaced in most industrialized countries by the basic oxygen process and the electric arc furnace, it nevertheless accounts for about one-sixth of all steel produced worldwide.

LOW-GRADE ORES

The transition to cheap steel did not take place without technical problems, one of the most difficult of which was the fact that most of the easily available low-grade iron ores in the world contain a proportion of phosphorus, which proved difficult to eliminate but which ruined any steel produced from them. The problem was solved by the British scientists S.G. Thomas and Percy Gilchrist, who invented the basic slag process, in which the furnace or converter was lined with an alkaline material with which the phosphorus could combine to produce a phosphatic slag; this, in turn, became an important raw material in the nascent artificial-fertilizer industry. The most important effect of this innovation was to make the extensive phosphoric ores available for exploitation. Among other things, therefore, it contributed significantly to the rise of the German heavy iron and steel industry.

MECHANICAL ENGINEERING

Closely linked with the iron and steel industry was the rise of mechanical engineering, brought about by the demand for steam engines and other large machines, and taking shape for the first time in the Soho workshop of Boulton and Watt in Birmingham, where the skills of the precision engineer, developed in manufacturing scientific instruments and small arms, were first applied to the construction of large industrial machinery. The engineering workshops that matured in the 19th century played a vital part in the increasing mechanization of industry and transport. Not only did they deliver the looms, locomotives, and other hardware in steadily growing quantities, but they also transformed the machine tools on which these machines were made.

The lathe became an all-metal, power-driven machine with a completely rigid base and a slide rest to hold the cutting tool, capable of more sustained and vastly more accurate work than the hand- or foot-operated wooden-framed lathes that preceded it. Drilling and slotting machines, milling and planing machines, and a steam hammer invented by James Nasmyth (an inverted vertical steam engine with the hammer on the lower end of the piston rod), were among the machines devised or improved from earlier

James Nasmyth invented the steam hammer, pictured above in his foundry near Manchester, Eng., for forging heavy pieces.

woodworking models by the new mechanical engineering industry.

After the middle of the 19th century, specialization within the machinery industry became more pronounced, as some manufacturers concentrated on vehicle production while others devoted themselves to the particular needs of industries such as coal mining, paper-making, and sugar refining. This movement toward greater specialization was accelerated by the establishment of mechanical engineering in the other industrial nations, especially in Germany, where electrical engineering and other new skills made rapid progress, and in the United States, where labor shortages encouraged the development of standardization and mass-production techniques in fields as widely separated as agricultural machinery, small arms, typewriters, and sewing machines.

Even before the coming of the bicycle, the automobile, and the airplane, therefore, the pattern of the modern engineering industry had been clearly established. The dramatic increases in engineering precision, represented by the machine designed by British mechanical engineer Sir Joseph Whitworth in 1856 for measuring to an accuracy of 0.000001 inch (even though such refinement was not necessary in everyday workshop practice), and the corresponding increase in the productive capacity of the engineering industry, acted as a continuing encouragement to further mechanical innovation.

CHEMICALS

The modern chemical industry was virtually called into being in order to develop more rapid bleaching techniques for the British cotton industry. Its first success came in the middle of the 18th century, when John Roebuck invented the method of mass producing sulfuric acid in lead chambers. The acid was used directly in bleaching, but it was also used in the production of more effective chlorine bleaches, and in the manufacture of bleaching powder, a process perfected by Charles Tennant at his St. Rollox factory in Glasgow in 1799. This product effectively met the requirements of the cotton-textile industry, and thereafter the chemical industry turned its attention to the needs of other industries, and particularly to the increasing demand for alkali in soap, glass, and a range of other manufacturing processes. The result was the successful establishment of the Leblanc soda process, patented by Nicolas Leblanc in France in 1791, for manufacturing sodium carbonate (soda) on a large scale; this remained the main alkali process used in Britain until the end of the 19th century, even though the Belgian Solvay process, which was considerably more economical, was replacing it elsewhere.

W.H. Perkin, at the Royal College of Chemistry in London, produced the first artificial dye from aniline in 1856. In the same period, the middle third of the 19th century, work on the qualities of cellulosic materials was leading to the development of high explosives such as nitrocellulose, nitroglycerine, and dynamite, while experiments with the solidification and extrusion of cellulosic liquids were producing the first plastics, such as celluloid, and the first artificial fibres, so-called artificial silk, or rayon. By the end of the century all these processes had become the bases for large chemical industries.

An important by-product of the expanding chemical industry was the manufacture of a widening range of medicinal and pharmaceutical materials as medical knowledge increased and drugs began to play a constructive part in therapy. The period of the Industrial Revolution witnessed the first real progress in medical services since the ancient civilizations. Great advances in the sciences of anatomy and physiology had had remarkably little effect on medical practice. In 18th-century Britain, however, hospital provision increased in quantity although not invariably in quality, while a significant start was made in immunizing people against smallpox culminating in Edward Jenner's vaccination process of 1796, by which protection from the disease was provided by administering a dose of the much less virulent but related disease of cowpox. But it took many decades of use and further smallpox epidemics to secure its widespread adoption and

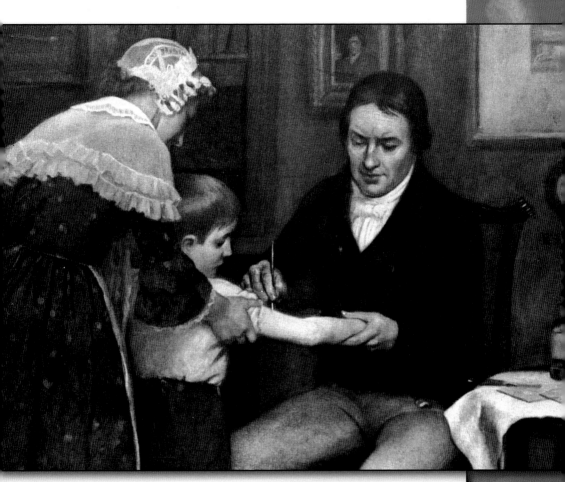

Edward Jenner administers a vaccine to a young boy. Jenner's revolutionary method of inoculation was not widely adopted right away.

thus to make it effective in controlling the disease. By this time Louis Pasteur and others had established the bacteriological origin of many common diseases and thereby helped to promote movements for better public health and immunization against many virulent diseases such as typhoid fever and diphtheria.

Parallel improvements in anesthetics (beginning with Sir Humphry Davy's discovery of nitrous oxide, or "laughing gas," in 1799) and antiseptics were making possible elaborate surgery, and by the end of the century X-rays and radiology were placing powerful new tools at the disposal of medical technology, while the use of synthetic drugs such as barbiturates and aspirin (acetylsalicylic acid) had become established.

AGRICULTURE

The agricultural improvements of the 18th century had been promoted by people whose industrial and commercial interests made them willing to experiment with new machines and processes to improve the productivity of their estates. Under the same sort of stimuli, agricultural improvement continued into the 19th century and was extended to food processing in Britain and elsewhere. The steam engine was not readily adapted for agricultural purposes, yet ways were found of harnessing it to threshing machines and even to plows by means of a cable between powerful traction engines pulling a plow across a field.

In the United States mechanization of agriculture began later than in Britain, but because of the comparative labor shortage it proceeded

Farmers harvest their crop with the aid of a McCormick reaper, invented by Cyrus McCormick.

more quickly and more thoroughly. The McCormick reaper and the combine harvester were both developed in the United States, as were barbed wire and the food-packing and canning industries, Chicago becoming the center for these processes.

The introduction of refrigeration techniques in the second half of the 19th century made it possible to convey meat from Australia and Argentina to European markets, and the same markets encouraged the growth of dairy farming and market gardening, with distant producers such as New Zealand able to send their butter in refrigerated ships to wherever in the world it could be sold.

CIVIL ENGINEERING

For large civil-engineering works, the heavy work of moving earth continued to depend throughout this period on human labor organized by building contractors. But the use of gunpowder, dynamite, and steam diggers helped to reduce this dependence toward the end of the 19th century, and the introduction of compressed air and hydraulic tools also contributed to the lightening of drudgery. The latter two inventions were important in other respects, such as in mining engineering and in the operation of lifts, lock gates, and cranes. The use of a tunneling shield, to allow a tunnel to be driven through soft or uncertain rock strata, was pioneered by Marc Brunel in the construction of the first tunnel underneath the Thames River in London (1825–42), and the technique was adopted elsewhere.

The Thames Tunnel utilized innovative tunneling shield technology to allow passage under the river.

The iron bell or caisson was introduced for working below water level in order to lay foundations for bridges or other structures, and bridge building made great advances with the perfecting of the suspension bridge—by the British engineers Thomas Telford and Isambard Kingdom Brunel and the German American engineer John Roebling—and the development of the truss bridge, first in timber, then in iron. Wrought iron gradually replaced cast iron as a bridge-building material, although several distinguished cast-iron bridges survive, such as that erected at Ironbridge in Shropshire between 1777 and 1779. The sections were cast at the Coalbrookdale furnace nearby and assembled by mortising and wedging on the model of a timber construction, without the use of bolts or rivets. The design was quickly superseded in other cast-iron bridges, but the bridge still stands as the first important structural use of cast iron.

Cast iron became very important in the framing of large buildings, the elegant Crystal Palace of 1851 being an outstanding example. This was designed by the ingenious gardener-turned-architect Sir Joseph Paxton on the model of a greenhouse that he had built on the Chatsworth estate of the duke of Devonshire.

Marc Brunel patented a tunneling shield for his plans to build an under-water tunnel in Russia. His invention inspired the tunneling shields used in construction of the London Underground subway system.

Its cast-iron beams were manufactured by three different firms and tested for size and strength on the site.

By the end of the 19th century, however, steel was beginning to replace cast iron as well as wrought iron, and reinforced concrete was being introduced. In water-supply and sewage-disposal works, civil engineering achieved some monumental successes, especially in the design of dams, which improved considerably in the period, and in long-distance piping and pumping.

With the onset of the Industrial Revolution and the development of powered machinery during the 18th and 19th centuries, much physical effort was gradually removed from work in factories and fields. Work was still regarded, however, as something

As the Industrial Revolution progressed, mass production increased thanks to the development of the assembly line.

separate from pleasure. The dichotomy between work and play persists even in today's highly industrialized society.

The world of work—comprising all interactions between workers and employers, organizations, and the work environment—is marked by the constant adaptation to changes in the technological, cultural, political, and economic environments. The study of historical changes in the organization of work can perhaps lead to a better understanding of the present problems—now on a worldwide scale—that accompany ongoing technical, political, and economic changes.

Most recently, industrial production has spread to developing countries. Economic and political questions of working-class and managerial relationships have altered on an international front, affecting political relationships on a global scale. Furthermore, new demands have been placed on educational systems in the developing countries as they attempt to train their workers for industrial production. Similarly, new demands have been placed on the educational systems of the developed countries as the older methods of organizing production, such as the assembly line, are being taken over by "smart" machines.

alkali Any of the univalent mostly basic metals of the group lithium, sodium, potassium, rubidium, cesium, and francium.

aqueduct An artificial channel for carrying flowing water.

artisan A person (as a carpenter) who works at a trade requiring skill with the hands.

Bessemer process The first method discovered for mass-producing steel.

cast iron An alloy of iron that contains 2 to 4 percent carbon, along with varying amounts of silicon and manganese and traces of impurities such as sulfur and phosphorus.

coke Gray porous lumps of fuel made by heating soft coal in a closed chamber until some of its gases have passed off.

commodity An economic good.

crucible A pot made of a heat-resistant material and used for holding a substance for treatment in a process that requires high temperature.

flying shuttle A weaving machine invented by John Kay that increased weaving speed.

guild A medieval association of merchants or craftsmen.

hydraulic Operated, moved, or effected by means of water.

Industrial Revolution The process of change from an agrarian, handicraft economy to one dominated by industry and machine manufacture.

ingot A mass of metal cast into a convenient shape for storage or transportation to be later processed.

labor Human activity that provides the goods or services in an economy.

laissez-faire A doctrine opposing governmental interference in economic affairs beyond the minimum necessary for the maintenance of peace and property rights.

metallurgy The science and technology of metals.

open-hearth process Also called the Siemens-Martin process, it is the steelmaking technique that for most of the 20th century accounted for the major part of all steel made in the world.

ore A mineral containing a constituent for which it is mined and worked.

production The making of goods available for human wants.

reverberatory furnace A furnace used for smelting or refining in which the fuel is not in direct contact with the ore but heats it by a flame blown over it from another chamber, the open-hearth process in steelmaking.

slag A by-product formed in smelting, welding, and other metallurgical and combustion processes from impurities in the metals or ores being treated.

smelt To melt or fuse (as ore) usually in order to separate the metal.

spinning jenny An early multiple-spindle machine patented by James Hargreaves for spinning wool or cotton

steam engine A machine using steam power to perform mechanical work through the agency of heat.

wrought iron The commercial form of iron that is tough, malleable, and relatively soft, contains less than 0.3 percent and usually less than 0.1 percent carbon, and carries 1 or 2 percent of slag mechanically mixed with it.

Hamilton Museum of Steam and Technology
900 Woodward Ave.
Hamilton, ON L8H 7N2
Canada
(905) 546-4797
Website: http://www.hamilton.ca/
    CultureandRecreation/Arts_Culture_
    And_Museums/HamiltonCivicMuseums/
    SteamMuseum
This museum focuses on the social and
    mechanical life of Canada's early industrial
    revolution. Housed in a 150-year-old water-
    works, this National Historic Site preserves
    two 70-ton steam engines, perhaps the old-
    est surviving Canadian-built engines.

MIT Museum
265 Massachusetts Avenue
Building N51
Cambridge, MA 02139
(617) 253-5927
Website: http://web.mit.edu/museum
The MIT Museum is dedicated to collecting,
    preserving, and exhibiting materials that
    serve as a resource for the study and inter-
    pretation of the intellectual, educational,
    and social history of the Massachusetts
    Institute of Technology and its role in

the development of modern science and technology.

National Museum of American History
14th Street and Constitution Avenue NW
Washington, DC 20001
(202) 633-1000
Website: http://www.americanhistory.si.edu
The National Museum of American History features a substantial collection of tools, machines, and other artifacts devoted to industry and manufacturing in the United States.

National Railroad Museum
2285 S. Broadway
Green Bay, WI 54304
(920) 437-7623
Website: http://www.nationalrrmuseum.org
With an extensive collection of railroad objects, photographs, manuscripts, and rolling stock, the National Railroad Museum provides interactive exhibits and innovative programs to encourage learning in the arts and history as well as STEM fields.

New York Hall of Science (NYSCI)
47-01 111th St.

Corona, NY 11368
(718) 699-0005
Website: http://nysci.org
NYSCI is a hands-on, energetic educational
experience where you can indulge your curi-
osity and nurture your creativity. NYSCI
offers professional development for teach-
ers, produces curricula and resources for
classrooms, and studies how technology,
gaming, and play affect how we learn.

The Tech Museum of Innovation
201 South Market Street
San Jose, CA 95113
(408) 294-8324
Website: https://www.thetech.org
The Tech Museum of Innovation allows those
who walk through its doors to find the tools,
spaces, and inspiration that they need to
unleash the innovator in them.

Thomas Edison Center at Menlo Park
37 Christie Street, Edison, NJ 08820
(732) 549-3299
Website: http://www.menloparkmuseum.org
The Thomas Edison Center educates the public
about Edison, his significant accomplish-
ments at this site, and his impact on modern
research and development.

Victoria and Albert Museum
Cromwell Road
London SW7 2RL
England
+44 20 7942 2000
Website: http://www.vam.ac.uk/page/i/
    industrial-revolution
The Victoria and Albert Museum features
    an exhibit on the Industrial Revolution
    in Britain, as well as a robust companion
    website.

WEBSITES

Because of the changing nature of Internet
links, Rosen Publishing has developed an
online list of websites related to the subject
of this book. This site is updated regularly.
Please use this link to access this list:

http://www.rosenlinks.com/TECH/Ind

For Further Reading

Grayson, Robert. *The U.S. Industrial Revolution*. Edina, MN: Abdo Publishing, 2011.

Hillstrom, Kevin. *The Industrial Revolution*. Detroit, MI: Lucent Books, 2009.

Hollar, Sherman. *Pioneers of the Industrial Revolution*. New York, NY: Britannica Educational Publishing, 2013.

Kramer, Barbara. *Thomas Edison*. Washington, DC: National Geographic, 2014.

McCormick, Anita Louise. *The Industrial Revolution in United States History*. Berkeley Heights, NJ: Enslow Publishing, 2014.

McDaniel, Melissa. *The Industrial Revolution*. New York, NY: Children's Press, 2012.

Mooney, Carla and Jen Vaughn. *The Industrial Revolution: Investigating How Science and Technology Changed the World*. White River Junction, VT: Nomad Press, 2011.

Morrison, Heather. *Inventors of Health and Medical Technology*. New York, NY: Cavendish Square Publishing, 2016.

Morrison, Heather. *Inventors of Transportation Technology*. New York, NY: Cavendish Square Publishing, 2015.

Mullenbach, Cheryl. *The Industrial Revolution for Kids*. Chicago, IL: Chicago Review Press, 2014.

Royston, Angela. *Inventors Who Changed the World*. New York, NY: Crabtree Publishing, 2011.

Samuels, Charlie. *Timeline of the Industrial Revolution*. New York, NY: Gareth Stevens Publishing, 2010.

Staton, Hillarie N. *The Industrial Revolution*. New York, NY: Kingfisher, 2012.

Van Zee, Amy. *The Rise of Industry, 1870–1900*. Minneapolis, MN: ABDO Publishing Company, 2014.

Wolfe, James. *The Industrial Revolution: Steam and Steel*. New York, NY: Britannica Educational Publishing, 2016.